Cello Time Runners

Cello accompaniment book

Kathy and David Blackwell

OXFORD

UNIVERSITY PRESS

OXFORD
UNIVERSITY PRESS

Great Clarendon Street, Oxford OX2 6DP,
United Kingdom

Oxford University Press is a department of the University of Oxford.
It furthers the University's objective of excellence in research, scholarship,
and education by publishing worldwide. Oxford is a registered trade mark of
Oxford University Press in the UK and in certain other countries

ISBN 978-019-356607-1

Cover illustration by Martin Remphry

Music and text origination Julia Bovee
Printed in Great Britain

Contents

1. Start the show

(for Clare)

KB & DB

2. Banyan tree

Jamaican folk tune

3. Heat haze

KB & DB

Easy going

4. Medieval tale

KB & DB

5. Chase in the dark

KB & DB

6. Spy movie

7. Romani band

KB & DB

8. Busy day

Busily

KB & DB

9. On the go!

KB & DB

12. Mean street chase

KB & DB

10. That's how it goes!

KB & DB

11. Blue whale

13. Allegretto

Mozart

14. Cornish May song

Cornish folk tune

15. Noël

Daquin

16. Prelude from 'Te Deum'

Charpentier

17. Paris café

KB & DB

18. Starry night

KB & DB

19. Cello Time rag

KB & DB

20. Caribbean sunshine

Calypso

KB & DB

21. Jacob's dance

KB & DB

22. Song from the show: page 30

23. The road to Donegal

KB & DB

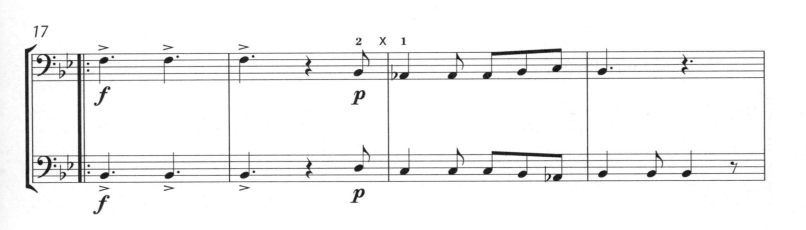

Can also be bowed (♩ ♪ ♩ ♪) etc.

24. Cat's eyes

22. Song from the show

25. Mexican fiesta

KB & DB

26. Summer evening

Flowing

KB & DB

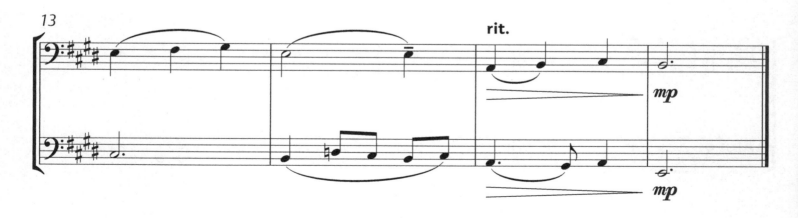

27. Extension rock

KB & DB

28. Show off!

Funky

KB & DB

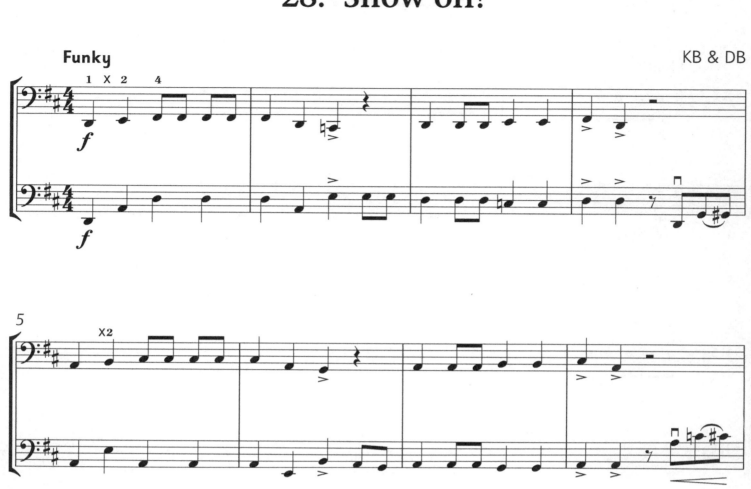

29. You and me

30. One day

31. Aerobics

Fast!

KB & DB

32. Hungarian folk dance

KB & DB

33. Show stopper

34. Farewell to Skye

(for Iain)

KB & DB

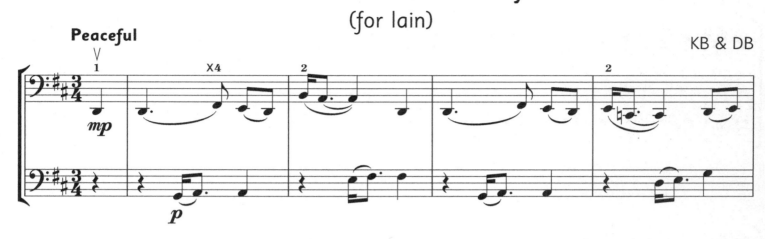